The Four Deadly Horsemen

(Terror, Bewilderment, Frustration, and Fear)

By Brandt R. Schubbe

2

Table of Contents:

4

The Four Deadly Horsemen

To: The Paul Dumas and The Betsy Barta for being shining examples of following my dreams. For that, I thank you.

Intro:

Dreamer came to a spot in his life where love lost took him into a
psychotic episode and his entries speak for themselves. He broke out
of it after years of therapy and many hours of sitting on his couch
with his cat. His dream is that his story will reach someone in a jail
cell or a psychiatric hospital or a treatment center, and not change
them, but help them realize that there really not alone.

1.

Terror:

There comes a moment in the chaos or after the chaos, that you look back or you look up, and you see how finished you really are, and they to me is terror. There is nothing in that moment that can bring you away from that point. You just have to cut through the murk until something elsewhere saves you.

AfterWar:

Pour that dream upon me
I need it now more than
I have ever needed it

I lost something in that war
More than my limb they
Call my left leg

I have no more desire
To keep on, and
What was it for

This life of,
People hating,
Hurting, lying,
And dying together

It is like the battle
Never ended, and
For me, it has
Just begun

Already Dead:

I always knew
I would decide
To bite the bullet

Little did I know
That is wouldn't
Be by my own hands

The cancer I have
Is not from cigarettes
But, from heredity

I could fight it
Like I have for
Year, but I wont

I haven't the
Strength in me

The pain is plenty
No more

I don't want it
Let me go
I have

An early twenties revelation:

Give me space
Space to think
I have a lot going on
It is to overwhelming
To have you
Barking orders at me

I must focus
For this moment
Is just right

In the dust of the road
That I covered my
Rear
There is a glimmer
Of a dream
That never left me
Even in my new
Adult life

The blue of the sky

Above me

Has the calmness
Of my future life
That I can
Not yet
Begin to see

All the soft whiteness
Of the marshmallow

The Four Deadly Horsemen

The Four Deadly Horsemen

I devour has
The sweetness
Of my innocents
That only
Others can see

I am the only one
That is lost
To me
All other have
Found me

Angry White Boy:

My attitude is
Like a rough rock

I never allow any
Single person to
Arrive closer than
I feel comfort

I die at the sight
Of a pretty woman

In the day, I do
My best never
To show my
Sad feelings

I lost the sight
I had as a child

Down by the river
I take a fishing pole

And hide from all
Never catch a thing

My mind alone
Is never enough

Out on the plank,
Of a ship, I step
And I look down
And I never jump

The Four Deadly Horsemen

The Four Deadly Horsemen

List after list
Nothing is shown

Now I sit alone
In the ocean
Away from all
And I deal with me

This has been a
Very long journey

Bad Boneyard:

Bones crumble onto
The floor
There they try to
Not notice the blood
That was before them

Inside the bones are
Secret memories of
The soul
Only to be remembered
By the dead

Bones don't just feel
The breaking

Each person who has
Known who the bone
Belonged to
Are felt as the bones
Break

So go ahead burn

That bone, but
Realize you are
Crushing all
Hopes and dream

Listen as the fire
Flares and fills in
The ashes

The Four Deadly Horsemen

The Four Deadly Horsemen

Feel the bitter
Taste of loss

Bed, Head, Dead, and Fed:

When the night fades
Into daylight, it is time
To fall into bed

As the noise is made
I let it pass
Into a slumber
It all passes my head

My cat tries to wake me
She needs to be fed
If she doesn't eat
She will fall dead

And so I take a rest
From my rest and
Feed my big girl
I watch her eat
And she is now fed

I go back into the

Bed

I put my hand under my
Head

The bugs bite me but I kill them
Dead

I rest long enough until it is time to be
fed

The Four Deadly Horsemen

Blood Pirates:

Children in the deep
Dead sea
All float in hope
That they will be rescued

Nobody is even looking
For them, for they are dismembered

In the land days
They fought all
The other children
And ate their
Corpses

Now they are gone
And one will only
Wish for them to
Never arrive back

Blood soaks the water
Breathing is unbearable

Boats wreck in the
Movement and
Only the ship
Wrecked realize
The torture in the sea

Many die, but
The few that did
Survive only wish
They were dead

Captured by pirates
The deep children and
The survivors, all
Are put to work
In a land
That is not
Known

As the years go by,
The children lose
Eyes, hands, and feet
Yet stay alive

The survivors are
Thrown into fire
Only to feel the
Forever pain

There is no
One coming
All are lost
To the events

All grown up,
The children
Enter the fire

Some only can
Feel, but not
Hear or see
Or even taste
Or smell,
But they will
Always feel

The Four Deadly Horsemen

The Four Deadly Horsemen

As the bloody water
Gets deeper

So do the new children

There is more and
More survivors

All are rescued by
Pirates, who do
Their best to
Make sure the
Pain is continued

And then one day
All is blood
And the pirates are
But, the last to enter
The fire
Now all burn
And can only
feel

Blood Soaked Sky:

In the madness
I stay, and
It took me to
The greatest beyond

Under the bridge
There was a man
Standing by a
Trash can filled
With fire

All over the
Ground was
Covered in
Trash from
Litterers

The water by
All, was filled
With shit from
People bathing

The smell from
The power plant
Transcended the
Mood of all whom
Were passing

The sound above
Were tires from
Cars passing by

The Four Deadly Horsemen

The Four Deadly Horsemen

On the bridge

I laid and
Looked out
At the red
Soaked sky

There was blood
In heaven, bleeding
Out of all who
Resided

I never left

That bridge

It is forever
With and for
My family and I

Bloody Waters:

Can you hear me
As you bask in
The glory of the holy

Under the stars
We are all mankind

There is none
Greater than
Another

Men who eat men
Are destined to
Be alone

Women who sleep with women
Are meant never to have children

They who die by
Their own hands
Know suffering

Like no other

Dreams of blood
Turned from water
Allow for the
Untrue to become
Forever true

Understanding ones
Deepest desires
The Four Deadly Horsemen

The Four Deadly Horsemen

Is the only
Freedom allowed

So go down
To the belly
Of the
Wicked

Touch all the
Not true

Desire what is

Untouchable

Drink up all
The blood

Become drunk
With fear

Never return
Of drift
Farther away

For enough
To never again
Be seen by
Another who
Will be against
All that you are

Building my tomb:

Constantly I hear a hammer pounding
I am sitting here waiting for my casket
To be made after all the others are built

All the feet of built wood to conform a grave
Many pass by and buy a piece for their loved ones
Will I have a loved one buy a casket for my body

I can only dream of a nice burial
Will I be conscious to see all the people
I know there will be at least fifty at the moment

Some times a family will burn the ashes
The ashes will either be held in a urn
Or flown out to a beautiful landscape

If I had my choice I would get a casket
And after I am buried to the ground I
Would prefer bugs to eat my flesh

I don't know where my burial plot will be,
But if I could choose it would be in the garden
Behind my parents out where I played football
If I die today bury my in a casket
Make is an unpainted casket
I want to go out easy

The Four Deadly Horsemen

2.

Bewilderment: Then there is that moment when you make no sense. It means the trust you have to rely on is on only the ground that your feet are on. Then when that shifts and things fall from the sky, you have nothing to trust. It is true misery.

Cocaine Dream:

Cocaine couldn't
Be that brilliant
Many have
Most have
Either quit
Or died

I remember as,
A boy
Glorifying the
Idea of being
A businessman
High on cocaine

I realize now
It isn't possible
I couldn't even
Drink my way
Through high school
I had to stop
Just to graduate

But, part of me
Thinks that
Perhaps cocaine
Could be
Manageable

I guess it is
Just something
I will have to
Live with

Crossfire Junction:

Of all this excitement,
I just want you to
Hold on

It's going to be chaotic,
The disease will spread
Oceans of people
Will exit

As it is decided,
As to who will
Stay or who will not

The world will welter
In the sun

Oceans will flood
All the lands

Boats will become
Preferred

Get yourself
Buckled in
It will be an
Eternity

When we meet again
Look in my eyes
And I will tell you
Where I've been

The Four Deadly Horsemen

Dead Birds:

Watch me as I walk
Around all the dead birds

How they got here
I don't know

They are here
They always have been

Some are blue and
They cover the most ground

The yellow ones are in the middle
While the red and orange
Are spaced all around

I pick them up
Hoping that some
Will have a bit of life

They never come alive
In the time I am allowed

This has been a year
That I have done this

I will stop someday
When I find a bird alive

If it never happens
Then I will never leave

Dead Boy Too Sad:

When God comes raging
In to you,
Don't forget what you
Were when you went
Down that alley
And saw her lying
On her last leg

You took that
Sandy blonde
Woman and
Ravished her

Now she lies
Dead up against
The red brick building

When you feel all that
Pity from all the lonely nights
Remember what you took
From that boy
In the garden
By the rhubarb

He was smiling
At you as his
Older cousin
You ripped off
His pants
And took him
To bloody beyond

While you are sharing a
Cell with Big Bob

The Four Deadly Horsemen

The Four Deadly Horsemen

Remember what you
Did to your father

How you cut his head
In half with a hatchet

He was giving you
A lecture about
Being honest
And you stole
His soul

When you are stalled
In a isolated cell in
White cement
Forget all you did
And you will
Never be forgotten

As you drift
Sigh in desperation
For you light
Is vanquished

Dead Dream Land:

As I wander around
In a land of Gods and Goddesses
I see my little way of going

There is a land we
Do not see
It is there helping us
As we ramble around

The big monsters are
Always behind our back
Waiting for a moment
When we die

What is not seen will
Again be seen

It will show all
And nothing ever will
Change what is our call
We will be forever still

Dead Fish:

I sit alone
On this rock
With no sights
And no noises
And just feelings

I have memories of
Lost things and people

Now I left all,
Just to not feel loss

All I do is feel loss
And I never feel complete

I had nostalgia the first few days
That time is past now
Only followed by isolation

If I died no one would know
Only me, and my thoughts

This is what I wanted
This is what I get

I could turn around,
And go back to it all
But, it is to late

I have gone full barrel
Into this thing

Now I look at my hook

34

And my fillet knife

I wonder what I will catch first
A fish or my wrist

The Four Deadly Horsemen

Dead in the Center of the Heart:

I saw her
Facebook status
The other day

She is now
Engaged

I lost her now,
And perhaps forever

Part of me is
Now dead,
And gone

I seem where
She was in my
Heart

It has a vacancy
And with that
I have hope

Dead Love:

I out witted her,
At least that is for sure

I never lied, but
I showed her I
Would be the
One who cried

She could not overcome
My sensitivity, but that
Was her weakness
For to her I have come

I would die for her life
In that she stuck me
With a sharp knife

I lay here dead
My blood dark red

Now, unlike her, I
Will die with her
In my eye

Dead Uncle Ed:

In and out of jail
My uncle has scars
On his body and
In his heart

I look in my uncles
Deep dark eyes
I wonder what he thinks
But, he never says a word

In his rest he worships
His mother and father
And all they have
With each other

My other uncles have
Forgotten him and all
He gave in his time
Of growing old

My uncle served in
The military
Just like my dad
Who passed already

My uncle is the
Closest thing I
Have to my father
And he is as good as dead

Dealing With a Dead Wife:

Lost in the moment
Away for a minute

Cherished by many
In the early years

It hits me hard to
Believe we are through

All the time we spent
Talking about the future
Has disappeared and went

Oceans couldn't separate
Us for we were for one
Another in this life, desperate

Go now, be with him
For I need you to
Be with him
My friend

The Four Deadly Horsemen

Dear Dead Friend:

I bet you never cried after we met
In the morning, following our last meeting
I cried, and wanted to be the one who died

Did you go soft
Or was is an aggressive death

All the blood
It seemed unreal

But, I will forget that
For I remember your smile

It lifts me everyday
And I know you
Would want me
To be okay

I owe you that
And nothing less

Death Dream:

The slow traveler
Is lonely in
His travels

He speaks to
No man or woman

He answers to no one
And no one seeks him

He left his stationary life
For a less desired life

As he goes about,
He dreams of dying

His belief is that he
Will see her again

As soon as his life
Is turned over

Death Mark:

We see that
There is an
Ageless angel

It carries us away
After our light is dimmed

The way we go, is
What we deserve

Lost is space
Far from it all

We are found by
A relic of our past

Joined by an armless army
Gathered by an aimless archer

We are the witnesses of
All the evils anywhere

In our report to the supreme
We ask for nothing, but
For another moment

Grace serves our need
Hate is dismissed for compassion

It never begin
Nor ends

Death of Sally Fields:

Her life, was
Spent thinking
About the cause
Of her living

As she bought flowers
Ever Sunday morning
Her tears made showers
She realized she was dying

Her hear gave out
At sixty-eight
Her one fried did shout
No one knew it was her fait

When they see her grave
They think of it as grave
Some grieve
Some never leave

Death Ripple:

The dead
Speak with
The wind

As the trees
Blow, the dead
Are communicating

To listen is
Divine, but
Few can handle
What is discussed

When one finds
A ripple in the
Water, he sees
His moment to
Die

It would only be
Cheating, if you
Denied that chance
To be gone

Deep Embedded Web:

The bitter bite of a spider
Erodes into the skin
Leaving a deep crevasse

The blood is blundered
The hole digs deeper
The pain is worsened

All I need is a shot,
But I am nowhere near
A spot to be fixed

The gauze I put around my wound
Eventually becomes bloody

I am near losing a limb,
If not my life

I run into a spirit guide on the trail
He sees the blood
He unwraps my bandage
He unveils a hole the size of a quarter

He takes out a knife
He cuts off my lower arm
I scream for days

Then the pain is less
It is as if I am free

The man tells me,
You must go
You will be fine

The Four Deadly Horsemen

The Four Deadly Horsemen

I leave the man with a wrapped nub

I am handicapped

In the moment, I cried of the loss
Now I realize, it could have been worse

I made it back home
I live with a grudge

I have picked up a new hobby
I collect spiders
The little ones that spin webs in my home

I wish to never forget
The very thing that made me
Who I am

Each web is a reminder
Of how I was nearly lost to this world

I only hope I find the one
Who bit me
I will put him on my bed
I will have my way with it

Dispersed Dead:

The dead man awaits
His awakening

In the cold North
All the rain washes
Away all filth

All who die in
The lakes, make it
To the surface

Fear they do not
Hope for a disappearance
Is all they can dream

Families of the dead
Do not know that they
Will never see their
Loved ones again

As the fog permeates
So do all the
Northern dead

The deceased
Never sleep
Only fantasize
About rest

In the dead of
Winter, all are
Alone in a array
Of forest

The Four Deadly Horsemen

Drowned in Bodies:

I ripped out my soul tonight
It wasn't hard
It just leaped right out

All saw it but me
I closed my eyes
I didn't want to see it

A girl pissed on my left overs
She told me,
"It is the cost"

After all left
I was alone
In my presence

I was empty all around
Clouds came and
The world poured over me

I would have cried if I could
I would have sought hope, but
It wasn't in me

I got up and started walking
Nobody looked at me
There was nothing for them to see

Before I knew it I was covered
In glue
I was stuck

The glue webbed my movements

I tried to be loosened, but
It wasn't happening

The water pouring on to me
Turned into blood
It covered me until I could not breath

I drowned that time only
To be awoken in
A sea of bodies

I recognized some of the bodies
Famous ones, such as
Otis Redding
William Faulkner
Jackie Robinson
And close relatives, such as
My dad
My grandpa
My grandma
Other I did not recognize

I was them now
And
They were me

Deep inside me I
Felt not a thing
Only everlasting emptiness

The Four Deadly Horsemen

.

Drunk with Death:

Bring me home
I miss it so
Carry me across
The bridge

I know I am loose
Baggage, but
My mother will
Make it worth
Your wild

Where are you going
I have money
I have food
I have water
Where are you going

The blood has been
Seeping out of me
All these days
I just have a
Mile to go

I see water in
My barrel
It is well water
I am refreshed

When the next
People come
I will offer them
A drink

And they will
Be grateful
No people have came
Night is on me
I hear the coyotes
They come closer
Each minute

I am losing sight
I see illusions of
Men with black hats
They are eating each other
They have come to take me
And I will be eating them
And they will be eating me

Damn this well water
It is all I have
My legs don't work
I can't breath long with
My smoke filled lung

Take me black hat men
Perhaps you will treat me
As your own

"We Will!"

The Four Deadly Horsemen

Everlasting Dead:

When we are forever dead,
We will regret nothing at all

In the mourning of our lives
By the ones who loved us
We smile at how sad
The world has
Become

We were
Once giant in
A small world that
We could see, but there
Was little to see in our limits

We are alive now
That we know
What we wil

Always know
From Here on out

Joined by a thousand corpses
I am home, here and out

Followers End:

The gasp of her last breathe
Covered my ears

I looked in her eyes
As they went blank

No air could stop it
Your day has passed

In the later
I look at your photographs

I see your past
I see our life

In the city
In the country

Wind passes
Fire flares

Fields are plowed
Snow is plowed

I want you back
It is to late for you to know

I grab my belongings
I follow the wind

The breeze takes me
East to west

Joined by followers
The Four Deadly Horsemen

The Four Deadly Horsemen

I push them away

I act as you
In those last days

I continue
I grab my legs

I continue
I grab my arms

I fall
I get up

It all ends abruptly
With a car to far on the shoulder

I breathe my last breath
My eyes go blank

Four Seasons of Death:

There is a dead body on the ground
Its skull is caved in
Its eyes have been plucked out
Its arms are covered in stretch marks
It looks as though the body stopped moving
And got stuck in the snow
The swirling blizzard covers the body
People see the body,
But act as if its not there
It is an act of acceptance

There is a hung corpse in the apartment
I see it day and night
The eyes are bulged out
The arms are bloated
The neck is snapped
The summer heat adds a smell to the room
I act as though it isn't around
I accept the company of the dead corpse

Up against the leafless tree there leans a lifeless person
The eyes are closed by staples
The hands are nailed to the tree
The feet are wrapped with dead twigs
The stomach is gouged
The fall welcomes people to the area
The people walk by and admire the tree
The people neglect the dead body
The body is accepted as part of the tree

A bloated body lays on the shore of the pond
Its eyes are no more
The Four Deadly Horsemen

The Four Deadly Horsemen

Its hands are water logged
Its feet are water logged
The teeth are missing

The skin is yellow and blue
As life sprouts up in the spring
The body is overlooked for beauty
As people play near the pond
They see the person as atmosphere
The corpse is accepted as new life

Hageman Woods:

I carry a hatchet
Into the deep woody area
I call the family ravine

In the woods, we bury
Our loved ones

I have three ex wives
And two brother
In-laws

I built them each a
Engraved stone

The engravings have
Their names
Their favorite quotes
And how they died

My mother buried my
Father
His mother and father
Are beside him

I will have my mother

Buried next to him

Next to the gravesite
Is a shack built by
My mother father
We call it our earth home

The Four Deadly Horsemen

The Four Deadly Horsemen

I live in the earth home
During the winters

Some say it is a
Hazard risk

I say it is mine
That is where I
Will lie until I die

The Four Deadly Horsemen

3.

Frustration: This is when you become angry and fight with others and when there is no one to fight with you fight with your self. It is a losing battle because nothing fights back. There is nothing but concern and care for your safety.

Hidden in a hole:

Jack and Bill went up the hill
They isolated from their friends
The confided in each other
The saw a black hole on top of the hill
Bill looked down
Jack pushed bill in the hole
Jack jumped down to be with Bill

In the hole Jack and Bill laid with broken limbs
The saw the sunshine from time to time
They had no escape
People avoided the hill with the hole
Bones were in the hole
It was a cemetery for dead cats

Bill found a scull
Jack threw it out of the hole
"Throw the bones out."
It took the two days to get all
The bones out of the hole

When night came the cold struck the men
They held each other
After some time they became delirious
They looked at the moon and thought
They had already died
It wasn't yet
"Kiss me on the lips
Bill kissed Jack
Jack felt a tingling sensation
Bill touched Bills body
Their clothes fell on the ground
In the night they laid together naked

The Four Deadly Horsemen

The Four Deadly Horsemen

A morning came and onlookers came
They saw the two naked corpses
They laid dead
As they were pulled out
Each man had blood on his penis
Their wives had an understanding
"It makes sense"
The funerals were combined
Kids laughed
Adults chuckled

"Someone had to fill the hole."

I am free to die:

I haven't done a whole lot
Since that cold winter night

The blizzard was pounding my car
I couldn't see, even the child I hit

Now, free by court
I am imprisoned

I am from Hell:

Look at me
I am hanging
From a noose
In your closet

Look at me
My wrists are cut
I have bled out

Look at me
I have a bullet
In my head
My skull is fractured

Look at me
I am at the
Bottom of the sea
With a chain wrapping
Around my neck

You may think
Me foolish,
To do
What I have
Done

You may think
Life is worth
Living

But obviously
I do not
Agree

I am The Devil:

When I meet my maker
I will give him a swat of
A handshake, and ask him
For a bit of chewing tobacco

As we sit and wait for
My judgment, I will
Demand for an appeal
Before a ruling is stated

I never will give in
That isn't how he
Decided to make me

With all my vigor
I will take his throne
I will demand for all
The damned

When he is lying
At my feet being
A beggar
I will spit in his
Eyes and mouth

When it all turns
Black and white
I will paint in color

I will isolate for
Five generations

When I go to seek
People, I will go

The Four Deadly Horsemen

The Four Deadly Horsemen

To the ones that

Did the worst
And I will drink
Their wine

Heaven will be
Turned into an

Apparent hell

Believers will shriek
When they die
And only then
Will there actually
Be a honest fear
Of death

I Killed My Life:

Here we go again
Away in a hurry

We never say good bye
We say, have a good day

You can't get the truth
Even if you ever tried

I am lost in a come again
Way of coming to believe

As the days pass
There is things
I miss, that came
My way and left

All the seasons seem special
All the women weep wildly

My family flew away
Years ago, and only
Told me to pray
Until the day when
They would be back

I am near death now
Cut in the gut by a
Man who called him
Self the devil

He laughed as I fell
To the ground

The Four Deadly Horsemen

The Four Deadly Horsemen

And now I have no
Way of reaching
Another soul that I
Met a ways back

The meaning of all
This is that I no longer
Have to run
I can now wait
And when I am found
It will be to late

Imagine a Hell:

One thing is certain
I will die
How?
I don't know,
But someday
When I least want it
I will become dead

At that point
I don't know if
I will be able
To do anything
But, I will be certain
I will never again
Be live

In death there is
So much uncertainty
Could I be with a Jesus?
Could I be in a dream state?
Could I be in fire?
Could I be in darkness?

I don't know, but
I do know that
Anything the same
For an eternity
Would be hell

If I am to be in a
So-called heaven
With white cloaks
And angel wings

The Four Deadly Horsemen

The Four Deadly Horsemen

I hope there is a
Substance called

Liquor or weed or smack
I mean if I will never
Be alive again
I hope to have a little fun
Or even to much fun

If I will be dead then
Let me fight demons
Give me a task
Something to kill
Off my ever reaching fear
Of the mundane
If I burn for an eternity
I shall have hope
A hope that there will
Be a drop of water
That hope would
Be better than an
Eternity with
Angel wings
And no dope

If I am in darkness
For an eternity
Let there be a desire
To see light
With a desire there
Is a feeling that
Darkness is better than

An eternity with
Angel wings
And no dope

The best case scenario
Is that it is a dream state
And nothing to wake up to
Just be and believe I am alive
At worse I will be in a
Nightmare, but
Some would say
I am already there

The Four Deadly Horsemen

Laura Lee's Inheritance:

Laura Lee you
I hope are free

I saw you one day
We were one together

I laughed with you
As the music played

We drank a beer together
Only to lose each other forever

We drifted apart and
Many walls stood between us

I hit you once
You forgave me

I gossiped about you once
You forgave me

Then we never saw each other
Ever again

It was my sixteenth birthday
And the news came shouting

On the radio a sixteen year old girl
Was chopped up by her mother

It was you
They found in Iowa

Your mother tried to run,

But she carried you with her

Years later I wonder
How had you forgave me

Years later I wonder
If I can ever forgive your mother

Laura Lee
If I may call you that

I will remember you

Letter from a dead Co-founder of Alcoholics Anonymous:

Dear Liz Norton,

I had a nightmare
You were hung in a closet
Previously four men
We both knew
Had their way with you

It was on our California vacation
Where all of our crew was living
Vicarious lives

I saw your face for the last time
And cried to a prayer,
Which I asked God
To take you away from me

He did so,
And we were apart
We never saw one another again

It is right
I feel well now,
In the next moment
I will die
Thinking of you

If what you preached is right,
I will stay away from the drink
I will live a long life
Without you

Sincerely,

Bill Wilson

The Four Deadly Horsemen

Letter from a dead dad:

I see the red in your eyes
The tears have fallen
It is for me you weep
I wish for you to sleep
This pain away, but I
Can't make you do it

All I had for you is now gone
All you had for me is still alive
Look in the drawer where I
Kept all the tools
There you will find a little
Wooden box

On the wooden box is
A white tulip preserved
Inside the wooden box
Is a gift of what you wanted
It is a ring
I wanted to give it to you,
But I feel to a dark coma
After that car hit me
While I was running to
Our child's birth

I miss you and
I regret that my child
Will have the same fait
As me, living with a
Dead dad, but I met
You, and you will meet
A man who will love you
And our son will meet a

Lover like you

With that ring,
I want you to give
It to our son, for when
He meets his love,
It is what my father
Left me, and now I
Leave it for him

I will see you, and
Tell our son that
I watch you both

Letter from a Dead Poet:

Dear Rachael,

I killed myself
At the off chance
We might see
Each other again

I never wanted to be
In your sight

I hate you so much
But, I could never dream
Of you dying because
Of me
I want your burden to
Be my death

Look at your life
And all the paintings
You produced

Look at my life
And all the poems
I wrote

We could have been
Something
But you forgot
I was around

You never even liked me
I only wanted to like you

I am gone now,

78

And for that

You owe the world

Letter from a Dead Priest:

Dear Caroline,

You make me want to bleed out
I want to slit my wrists and
Bleed out

I wouldn't though
I can't put that burden on you

If I die it shall be natural
No cause of my own

If what you preached is true
I will be with Jesus

When I die

I have seen him in a dream
His hand was up with glory
He was smiling from
Cheek to cheek

If I see you again,
I hope you are with a man
It does not matter who he is
As long as it isn't me

Sincerely

Ezekiel

80

The Four Deadly Horsemen

4.

Fear: The last part, but the part that encompasses all decision making in all this creation, and nothing can beat it but faith, and in this state fear always wins.

82

Lonely Retirement:

I mismanaged my funds
Now I am broke with
Nothing to show
And no friends

The Four Deadly Horsemen

The Four Deadly Horsemen

Night with Satan:

Tear my clothes off
Ravish me in this night
I am yours
You are mine
Please don't take your time
Have me
Now

In the mirror I see you
Pounding me with all
Your mite
Strangle me
Cut me
Have my blood

Drip drip
My blue blood turned red
Is falling into you
We will be one
We will have lust
Trust in your thrust

I am losing breathe
You can have it
Breath me
Inherit my oxygen
I die for you
Only for this moment
This moment will
Never end

My conscious is lost
In you

I am now only yours
And only for an
eternity

The Four Deadly Horsemen

Oceans of Death:

The oceans are covered by blood
Some human, and some not so much
I swim all in the deep red
It wouldn't be as such
If I didn't

As I struggle for my last
Breathe

As I struggle for my last
Energy

As I struggle for my last
Hope

I see all my friends
In a picturesque memory

I cry with bliss
Over the people I've met

In this life
There is only one way
To die

That way is alone

Old Willow Yell:

We will make this right
It all began with a willow tree yelling
"Carry my will upon your shoulders."
All night it yelled
Only to be shut up

A bulldozer swept by and took it down
The willow tree cried
"O let this all end."
The whole time it happened
The people sleepless were annoyed

Little did they think
About anything, but their sleep
"Shut that damn tree up."
The whole block angered
By the tree

What is next, but a
Dead willow trying to be set free
The damage has been made
We see it all damn day
Then we set our bodies up on the branches

The kids come by and
All sit on the pitied willow tree
"Lets build a bench."
I gathered my tools
As did the kids

We built the strongest and
sturdiest of all benches
"This will do."
We sat all day and night

The Four Deadly Horsemen

The Four Deadly Horsemen

Up on the willow tree

It was the last thing
We could possibly do

One day to die:

As I drink
This cup of coffee
I blindly think
I desire to be
Listed as free

Tomorrow I ship
Away

I have enlisted only
To get away

Little did I know
That it would be
A lifetime

Either way
Tomorrow I die
Never free

At least as,
I am now

Teaching a Soldier how to Die:

Deep in the red water I wait for my end
It all came after a man found my note
I was lost to war, and the substance of
The later, contained secrets
It was considered treason
I let down my country
The writing, I will never send

I am not the first man to be caught
There were fifty more
They all were scalped by
Ten year olds
I was the leader of the men
They were in my unit
It was my letter that, led to the notice
This is not what I sought

I never intended for this
Why God?
What must I do?
When will this end?
Who are you to take these men?
How can I fix this?
I lean into my 2nd in command
I put my lips to his forehead
I give him a soft, gentle kiss

A wave comes through the water and the blood is swept away
All my men were swept away, and all the ten year old drowned
I stand up and look at all the soldiers
The guns point toward me
Lightning strikes down
Thunder rumbles
Wind blows

The guns are flown in the air
I am blown down stream

As I float I see the killers of my men swiped from this earth
I cry in joy for the repentance of my men
I believe I will be okay
The tide becomes stronger
I am swiped under the water
I can't move
I stay under the water
I am alive no longer

It is right now
We are all dead
There must have been no other way
We will be missed,
But by people who will never know what we did
That, I suppose, is right
We are gone, and that is how

The Four Deadly Horsemen

The Four Deadly Horsemen

Tenderloin Neighborhood:

A pig is a large creature
It does many things to feed America
It lives without complaint

A pig eats the waist, and
Likes it

A pig uses mud
To cool down

A pig stays is a closed space
All its life

Once a pig dies
It is for a cause

Once a pig dies
It has achieved parenthood

Once a pig dies
It is replaced by another

This animal can give a lesson
To humanity

Or humans can continue to
Not see the glory
Of the pig

The death of Bob Dylan:

"I got a death wish"

Hung in this noose
With a garbage pail
At my feet

"I make a prayer"

O, Maker look at me now
What have you made of me?
Your plan is lost to me
Grant me one thing
That thing may be
My child's mother

"I want to see her die"

She ratted me out
And for what
A peace of mind
She shall never have it

"I will be the first free"

As my neck dangles
I have passed into
The unknown
Now ask

"What will come of you all?"

The Four Deadly Horsemen

The Death of Grandma:

She wasn't to talkative
As she kept her words
To the ones that mattered

Alone she listened as
I cried, and spoke of
Trouble

In the company of others
She allowed me to feel
A part of her

Her children treated her as a queen
As she treated them like princes and princesses
Her king, their father was never
One to punish or even rule
They were fair royalty

As their ascendant, I have a duty
To treat the world as they all did

In this sad hour,
We all have lost
A great lady

She left us
Each other

The Deaths:

The obituary today
Had three people

One was eighteen
Another was forty
The last was eighty

Each one was a lady
Each died from
Health complication

My uncle told me once,
No matter who dies,
You will not be prepared

I assume all these ladies
Are missed by somebody

The Legacy of the Day after Christmas:

Strangers struggle to stream their small lives into mine
Joining in the jump to jump life
Walking willingly towards walls of blockage

In an incident, I met my maker
Joined at the hip, we wept tears of tattered lives
Tortured for our deeds, we continued to try

Understanding the effects of our efforts
Yelling from ear to ear
Scratching the surface of soft spoken people

Humming sweet symphonies for friends to follow
Drowning in damp blood of tragic endings
Forgetting where the fight took us

Confusion caused us to stay silent
Humor kept us from killing each other
Ever so eerie the trap that we were led to

We took fifty of our friends and
Were caught stealing our land back
When a clan took us from our path

On wood decks we stood
With ropes around our necks
Below our feet, trapped door

The door flipped open

Are feet ungrounded
Our necks snapped

Into death we went

Unknowing
Untouched
Unstopped

To the girl who killed me:

In the dead of evening
I will offer you a peace offering

I won't spit
I won't cut

We will be willing
To join each other
For a sip of coffee

Joined together
We will laugh

I will continue to look in you
At all the joy you bring to me

Laughter from others
Will annoy us

Crying from your mother
Will irritate us

Yelling from your father
Will enrage us

We will run
Into open field
Away from all people
Only to find we don't belong

We will return home
With our tails between
Our legs

We will try to make it last,
But is will be bitter

The time will pass
And we will lose our moment
We will be away from each other
In a much needed way

I will see you and wave,
But there will be nothing to say

You will see me as
A former love
I will see you as
The one that the
World took away

It is all as it should be
With us sharing time
To get to another time

Just remember if we
Never talk again
It is not personal

The Four Deadly Horsemen

The Four Deadly Horsemen

What is eating me:

I want the head
Put back on his body
What is the reason
To have a dad with no head
He can no longer shout at me
He can no longer cry for me
He can no longer see me
Give his head to me
I will sow it on his body
I will bring life to the man
You call my father
I have never seen this man,
But part of me is him
And part of him is me
Look at me
Do I look complete
I think not
I am a bastard

Wrapping head around death:

Oh, this moment
As I wish to die
Why am I so eager
To die

I only reminisce
My desires in
Close company

Pour man has to
Hear my only wish
And that is to die

This life is to slow
I hate the wait
In the end we all die
When will it come to
Me

As I wait I just
Continue to do
More than I have
Before

Joined by my fifty
Closest friends and
Family

Some would love to
Have all I do

I just want to die
In an act of violence
Or an act of illness

The Four Deadly Horsemen

The Four Deadly Horsemen

It doesn't matter how
I go

When it is done
We are all dead

The End.......

Manufactured by Amazon.ca
Bolton, ON